BOOK TITLE GENERATOR

A PROVEN SYSTEM IN NAMING YOUR BOOK

SCOTT LORENZ

WESTWIND BOOK MARKETING

INTRODUCTION

> *"No book has ever been bought that wasn't picked up, and to some extent, what makes you pick it up is the cover; it needs to immediately tell people that's the genre they love."*
> — James Patterson, Best-selling author

Your book needs to stand out from the competition.

Most authors understand that is a part of successful authoring in the 21st century, but there is a key component of that equation that is often overlooked.

Your book needs to have a strong title. Without a powerful title, your book, however well-written it might be, is destined to fall behind the competition.

What does that mean? It means you've got to think that title through. Easy enough, right? Not so fast.

Coming up with that just-right title is not as simple as it might seem, however. What makes one title outperform another in the terms of clicks, likes, and sales is oft-misunderstood.

Some authors want to believe they can make something up, slap it on the cover, and leave it at that. Whatever sounds snappy or catchy at that moment should be OK, right?

Wrong.

That approach may have worked ten years ago. Today, however, it simply is not realistic. Wherever your prospective reader is right now, they are likely being inundated with the covers and titles of literally thousands of books. They come as Amazon preferences. They show up as social media posts. They splash across full-page advertisements in print media.

Book publicists such as myself understand there are a lot of options out there and your title needs to cut through the noise.

What I'm talking about is the idea of discoverability. What is that? In the simplest possible terms, discoverability means doing everything possible to get your book in front of the right prospective readers, forcing them to take notice of you and your message.

There is a lot that goes into discoverability. The reality is that your book's title is an absolutely vital aspect of that discoverability formula.

That's what you want, right? A book that is easy for your prospective reader to find, one that jumps off the page or the screen and commands their attention.

I can show you how to do that. I can teach you tricks for titling your book in such a way that it stands out from the competition.

ABOUT THIS BOOK

Judging by the fact that you actually picked up this book, you understand how important applying proper book marketing techniques are to your overall publishing venture. Otherwise, you would have simply slapped on whatever title sounded good at the moment and been done with the whole thing. Congratulations, you are already one step ahead of the game.

The book you are reading now is the definitive guide to understanding what makes an effective book title. In the following pages, I will discuss specific areas and methods that, employed properly, will help draw attention to your book, give it the broadest audience possible, and convert into the only bottom line that really matters: sales.

In this book, I will cover a wide range of important topics related to book titles. Each chapter will be devoted to a distinct area.

Some of them will seem intuitive right off the bat. Others, however, will probably strike you as being out of left field. What do I mean by that?

For example, did you know that you can use profanity in a book title? In Chapter 9, I will cover how a number of successful authors rode their potty mouth all the way to the top of the bestseller list.

Subtitles are among the most important elements in a book's sales page presentation.

Did you know that Amazon gives you room for 200 characters in your title? That is a lot of real estate. Filling that space with an informative subtitle that is both keyword rich and enlightening will give you a leg up in overall searchability.

You probably understand what a book's genre is. If you're a fiction author, you had better understand the difference between a mystery and a thriller. But did you know that you can effectively "mash-up" book titles, creating a unique element of intrigue in your readers?

Writing in the nonfiction space? You're going to need to have a grasp of keywords. Specifically, what consumers of your topic enter into Amazon, Google, and whatever other search engine they use when they're looking for a solution to their problem. Adding those to your title is key, as search engines favor title text over descriptions. The point is, I am going to come at the topic of titling a book from a number of angles.

If at any point you would like my book marketing firm's help in promoting your book and creating your book title, please visit: http://www.book-marketing-expert.com where you can fill out our brief questionnaire telling us about your book, business and publishing goals.

THE CORRECT KEYWORDS

Among the first concepts you must master in order to create the right title for your book are keywords. You may have heard this term before in relation to web-based services like search engine optimization (SEO), but it applies to books as well.

Why? Because Amazon operates like a giant search engine. If you want your book to show up in those user searches, you need to make sure you're using the right keywords.

Without boring you, let me explain how this works.

Keywords are the words (or a string of words and terms creating a phrase) that Amazon users enter when searching for an item. If you want someone searching for an item like "car wax" to find your listing then you need to make certain the phrase "car wax" is somewhere in your product title.

That all sounds rather simple, right? Users know what car wax is. It's not mistakable for something else like candle wax or ear wax, so the connection comes without much difficulty.

This logic works for a great number of products beyond just car wax. I use car wax because it's clearly defined, but you could apply the logic anywhere. If you're selling printer ink, guitar strings, or a Funko Pop of Thanos from *The Avengers*, your keywords are relatively clear.

The trouble with keywords when it comes to books is that they often aren't as clear as other products. That is not mere speculation. Keywords are often more subjective when it comes to books, and another reality is that the Kindle Store is far more crowded than other places within Amazon.

These realities are how we get to the idea of finding the "right" keywords. Nailing keywords for your book is a science. Getting it right is crucial to the sale of your book.

SO, what makes a keyword for your book?

Among the most important keywords are those associated with your primary genre. If you write spooky books, let's say in the ever scorching-hot genre of paranormal romance, you're going to want to make sure the term "paranormal romance" is included somewhere in your subtitle. That way, readers searching for the term will more easily find your book.

Book keywords can become difficult when seemingly similar terms like "paranormal" and "supernatural" come into play. They mean the same thing, right? Many readers will use these similar terms interchangeably, making your task of coming up with the right title more challenging.

It is important you understand that there are differences in profitability too. While you might see those two terms as one and the same, your readers may not. If more people use "paranormal" than "supernatural," the former will lead to a larger potential audience.

There are methods you can use to find out what keywords are more profitable than others. The first method is do some basic sleuthing through Amazon on your own. Search for books similar to yours using your presumed genre. If you come up with a screen full of books that resemble yours, then you're on the right track. If you write hardboiled noir mystery and get a page full of cozies, you need to refine your search. Luckily, there are tools and websites out there that can help you streamline that search. In this arena, you don't want to stand out. Here, you want to fit in.

Another method is to look on the website goodreads.-com. It is a massive website made for readers to discuss, rate, and review books (. . . and just so you know, the website is owned by Amazon).

A clever way to utilize Goodreads is through "Listopia," its massive on-site collection of reader-curated book lists. These lists are a fantastic way to find your next good read in any category (keeping with the site's promise), but can also be an excellent resource for studying titles and search terms for books similar to yours. For example, if you were writing high fantasy and were interested in researching your genre, you could search out lists of books for people who liked *Game of Thrones*. Those lists would contain hundreds (maybe even thousands) of books in the category, with information ranging from keywords, covers and, of course, titles. Maybe the best part of Listopia is that it is reader-sourced, meaning these books are proven to have reached the same fans you're looking to impress.

Finding the right keyword is a bit like trying to predict buyer behavior. If you could really do that, a lot of your problems would be solved. But you can't, so you're going to need to do your homework.

ONCE YOU GET those basic keywords down, the next step is working them into your book's title listing. For example, if you've settled on "paranormal romance" as your genre for your debut novel *Once Bitten*, great, you're on the right track. You will need to find a logical way to work keywords in. What do I mean by logical?

Keyword stuffing (jamming in every possible word) doesn't work. For one thing, it looks unprofessional. On the level of search engine functionality, jamming a bunch of phrases into a listing has proven ineffective for increasing exposure. Yeah, the bots have caught on and caught up to us.

When you go about the task of entering your book title into the Amazon page you may want to consider something like:

Once Bitten: A Paranormal Romance.

Right away, the logical use of genre-based keywords does two things. First, it allows searches to differentiate between the *Once Bitten* book that falls into the cooking category, the one that's a memoir about being attacked by an angry snake, and yours. The other is that it announces its presence to readers.

Nailing the right keywords also comes later in your book's Amazon experience, too.

Keywords might not be as obvious as your genre title either. Keywords and search behavior are as wide and varied as anything else we humans do when we get in front of our computers. Keywords may include settings. Let's say you write World War II military thrillers. Readers of that niche are well-practiced in searching for that specific term. A book like that may want to add the subtitle, *A World War II Military Thriller.*

Your best keywords may end up drilling down deeper into the genre than just paranormal mystery, into a specific niche genre like urban fantasy or something else.

If you are writing a book series centered on a specific character, eventually their name will fall into the realm of logical keywords. Readers talk about characters. If senior heartthrob Jack Longtooth is going to serve as the hero of *Once Bitten* in the endless series of books, you may want to add that name as well. *Once Bitten: A Jack Longtooth Paranormal Mystery.*

The key to understanding keywords in titles is that they are there to complement your book's core title. On their own, words like *Once Bitten* can mean anything.

> *You need to make them mean what your targeted reader thinks they mean.*

IF YOU'RE STRUGGLING for the most effective keywords for your book, try using a Google search. For example, if your book is about Paris, enter that broad keyword into the search bar and Google will list a series of popular searches in its predictive text.

Paris tours. Paris hotels. Paris at night. Scrolling down, you will eventually find the one that fits.

Any one of these phrases could make an ideal cluster of keywords for your book's title. This method is especially effective because people across the world—your potential readers—informed Google. This wasn't something artificial. Rather than struggle with guesswork about what your search terms might be, use the world's most powerful search engine to tell you what they are.

USING **Additional Technology**

Besides using search engines such as Google and Bing and the platforms Amazon and Goodreads, some tech-savvy authors use software called Publisher Rocket (formerly known as KDP Rocket). Publisher Rocket analyzes all of Amazon, drumming up valuable data in areas like keywords and categories, and compares the profitability and level of competition for specific terms and words.

Best-selling author Michelle Kulp has discovered a number of interesting book-selling methods. She has figured out a way to use this software to get snappy titles that catch a reader's attention, all backed up by research using Publisher Rocket.

She cleverly enters the keywords of top selling books in her category on Amazon, and then uses some secret sauce to generate a title, subtitle, categories, and keywords. Michelle Kulp is the author of a dozen best-selling books including: *Backwards Book Launch: Reverse Engineer Your Book and Unlock Its Hidden 6-Figure Potential, Work From Home & Make 6-Figures: The Joy of Making More In Half the Time (Without the Hassles of a Job, Boss or Commute)*, and *How to Find Your Passion: 23 Questions That Can Change Your Entire Life*. By the way, her books are terrific!

Everyone knows that SEO (search engine optimization) is critical for businesses, but it's also critical for authors, not only on their websites, but on Amazon as well.

Wouldn't it be nice to know if people are searching a particular term or phrase covered in your book? Wouldn't you like to use the most-searched keyword in the title of your book? Heck yes!

My go-to webmaster Jeff Jacobs of Marketing Success builds top websites for all types of businesses, including authors. One of the tools he uses in getting a website ranked on Google and Bing costs hundreds of dollars a month. Obviously, that's way out of line for most mortals, so for the rest of us, he suggests "Keyword Surfer."

Check it out today; the service is completely free.

So, get technology on your side. Don't guess on a title. Use the software tools out there to help title your book.

#1 NEW YORK TIMES BESTSELLER

Mitch Albom

Author of the #1 New York Times bestseller
Have a Little Faith

the five people
you meet in heaven

THE INTERNATIONAL BESTSELLER
MIDNIGHT
IN THE
GARDEN OF
GOOD AND EVIL
JOHN BERENDT

Fifty
Shades
of Grey
E L James
#1 *New York Times* Bestseller

USING THE MOST POSSIBLE SPACE . .
. BUT DOING SO WISELY

"While some people meet their perfect partners during their teenage years and live happily ever after, the vast majority of us have to date lots of people before we find what we're looking for. The same holds true for titles. I suggest making a list of at least five different titles before deciding upon one. There's also much to be said for asking friends and family which title they prefer."
— Jacob M. Appel, *The Man Who Wouldn't Stand Up*, winner of the 2012 Dundee International Book Award

---

This follows closely on the heels of the previous chapter.

There is something important that you need to know about the line where you enter your book's title. You get up to two hundred spaces to title your book.

That's right, two hundred spaces.

If you think about it, there are few successful books

out there with really long titles. Think of books such as *The Curious Incident of the Dog in the Night-Time* which comes to a total of forty-eight spaces, or *The Man Who Mistook His Wife for a Hat* which is just thirty-eight.

However quirky and poetic they are, those are a pair of long, mouthful titles.

Those are the kinds of long and confusing titles I'm trying to steer you away from. Books such as these, although wildly successful, owe their prominent place in our culture's awareness for other key reasons. Namely, that they were written by established authors with massive, powerful publishing companies behind them. The first-time author, either working as an independent or coming out with a small publisher, needs a title that is clearer. They need to use that space efficiently, filling it with keyword-rich subtitles, the name of a signature character, or a series title.

Going back to our example of *Once Bitten*, those two words on their own don't mean anything. Maybe the cover depicts a hunky, vampire football-playing teenager, but thus far, Amazon's search engine doesn't take the title into consideration (I stress the "thus far" element here). Again, doing some research works.

Although our discussion largely centers on what works in the Amazon algorithm, we can still look to the major best seller lists like *The New York Times* and *USA Today* as well as online book aggregators like Goodreads. Those tell us that fiction titles are shorter than nonfiction titles. Fiction generally runs in the neighborhood of five words, while nonfiction commonly runs in the range of five to seven words.

What do I mean about using your allotted title space wisely? Quite simply that. When you're working on your book's title, it is important to work as many natural keywords as possible into the line. We've established that already. But jamming in every possible word is a sloppy scattershot approach that is rarely effective. Yet, people do it. If I see one more nonsensical fifteen-word book title with a ten-word subtitle, I'm gonna scream. Can you read it on a thumbnail on your phone? If not, you probably want to reconsider.

Can you read it on a thumbnail on your phone? If not, you probably want to reconsider.

Here is why that type of stuffing doesn't work: Your title is your entire book distilled down to a single word or phrase that must capture everything from its central ideas, your voice, the book's emotions, and perhaps in some cases, the value proposition. Ranging too wide, grasping at whatever sticks dilutes the emotion or poetry in a good title (discussed in future chapters) and replaces it with a mess.

THE INTERNATIONAL BESTSELLER
'HERE'S THE NEXT THE LOVELY BONES...A RARE BOOK' EVENING STANDARD
NOW A MAJOR MOTION PICTURE
The Time Traveler's Wife
AUDREY NIFFENEGGER
VINTAGE

JANET
#1 NEW YORK TIMES BESTSELLING AUTHOR
EVANOVICH
MOTOR
MOUTH
An Alexandra Barnaby Novel

If at any point you would like my book marketing firm's help in promoting your book and creating your book title, please visit: http://www.book-marketing-expert.com where you can fill out our brief questionnaire telling us about your book, business and publishing goals.

MASTERING THE USE OF EMOTIONAL WORDS

Think of your book's title as the headline for a breaking news story. For as long as newspapers (and now internet news content) have been around, diligent scribes have been searching their thesauruses for the right combination of power words for headlines as a way to draw readers' curiosity.

Compare and contrast these two headlines:

. . .

STOCKS FALL on Pandemic News

and

STOCK MARKET PLUMMETS Over Pandemic Fears

THESE TWO HEADLINES could both accurately describe the same series of events, right? If you read the articles about how the stock market had a bad day due to reports of a breaking public health crisis, you would deem them both accurate.

But accuracy is only half of the goal. Just one of these two headlines adequately captures the emotions associated with the story, though. That reality is owed to three synonymous words or phrases.

"Stock market" carries more weight than "stocks." Why? Because more broadly defining the location of the entire stock market instead of just stocks forces a natural question: Was *my* portfolio affected by this? That alone forces many readers to inquire.

A person or a thing can "fall" from any height. But when that same person or thing "plummets," we know immediately it is from on high and usually implies a tremendous crash at the end. Exchanging those synonyms gives us a grave sense.

The same with "news" versus "fears." News can be anything. It could mean that a cure was found, for all you know. The word fear seizes an emotional response, one you are knowingly transferring onto your reader.

A new term out there, "click bait," is widely used to

describe a type of news article where the only purpose is to get anxious readers to click on it and find out what on earth is going on. While this practice is regarded as reprehensible in news, accurately connected to patently false or misleading stories or conclusions, it works well for books.

Your title is the first barrier to a sales conversion.

You want that prospective reader to click the link, taking them to your book's page where they can actually buy the title. Take a moment to consult a list of popular fiction titles on Goodreads. You will find that almost every one of those at the top capitalizes on one or more strong emotional words.

The Hunger Games by Suzanne Collins. The idea and feeling of *hunger* touches on an essential need and drives it home with the emotion of fear. Any other word wouldn't accurately capture it.

To Kill A Mockingbird by Harper Lee. *Kill* stirs up feelings in anyone.

The Book Thief acts similarly. A *thief* conjures up strong associations of crime.

Your emotional words don't necessarily need to be negative. In some instances, you may want to consider warm and fuzzy or intriguing emotion.

One of the most effective emotional titles ever, *The Giving Tree,* by Shel Silverstein, grabs a prospective reader at their core need to feel connected to others.

The *DaVinci Code* by Dan Brown works on his

prospective reader's curiosity.

The list goes on and on, filled with emotionally stirring fiction titles. Luckily, Goodreads houses hundreds of book lists (curated both by the site and individual readers) where writers can do targeted title research. You can go into a list of the most popular books in a whole host of genres and find some very specific emotional words.

Back to the subject of genre. Each one capitalizes on a different array of emotions. Why? Because their loyal readers are looking for a different feeling. Horror readers want to be frightened; romance readers want to swoon. Different words get us to those ends.

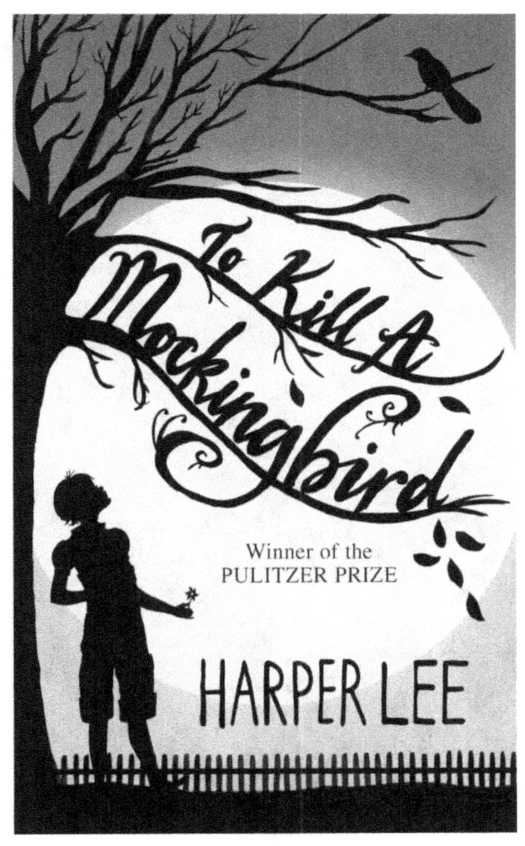

To Kill A Mockingbird
Winner of the
PULITZER PRIZE
HARPER LEE

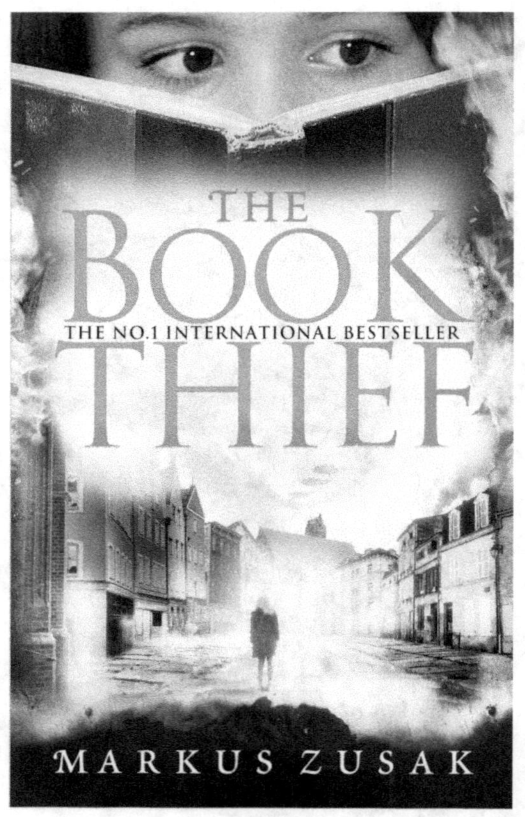

THE
BOOK
THE NO.1 INTERNATIONAL BESTSELLER
THIEF
MARKUS ZUSAK

ALLITERATION & POETRY

By and large, book readers are lovers of language. They desperately want to experience real emotions through your character's journey. These are the central reasons they're willing to spend their money to read your 70,000 words of fiction.

Why not capitalize on that love with a poetic or emotionally evocative title?

A number of successful books owe a great deal of their success to a well-crafted title. There are more than a few to choose from, but think of well-regarded books like *Everything I Never Told You* by Celeste Ng or *To Kill A*

Mockingbird by Harper Lee or *Midnight in The Garden of Good and Evil* by John Berendt. Each of these titles evokes a very specific feeling. In Ng's case it is one of emotion. The title plainly suggests a person who has kept a secret for a very long time. In Lee's classic, there are undertones of injustice and punishment.

There are a few interesting touchpoints in Berendt's classic of creative nonfiction. First off is the use of "midnight," hanging as the foreboding witching hour over the whole book. The word "garden" has two different connections; it can simply be a place for growth and renewal, or the Biblical Garden of Eden. Good and evil are the quintessential forces engaged in an epic clash for the human soul. There is no doubt that this book is going to travel to dark, thoughtful, and morally questionable places.

Whatever your preference, emotional words and poetic writing draw a reader's attention. Their use of language makes the concept sticky and easily memorable. Even in the age of Amazon, Goodreads, and social media, word of mouth is a critical element of your book's overall success.

EVEN SIMPLER THAN the idea of poetry is alliteration. Especially effective in children's literature, alliteration is a great way to draw attention to your book. Speaking of sticky—the repeated use of the same first letter through a series of words is almost guaranteed to make your book memorable.

Think of titles like *Gone Girl*, *Angela's Ashes*, *The Two Towers* and *Black Beauty*. Once those find their way into your mind, it's hard to mistake them for something else. It's very difficult for me to imagine someone getting a recommendation to read *Gone Girl* and then forgetting the title when they sit down to search for it online. Gone what? It makes no sense. You've heard it once—you remember it forever.

Another of my favorite alliterative titles is *Banjos, Boats and Butt-Dialing,* a book by humorist Mike Ball in his "What I've Learned" series. It captures everything you need to know about the book and its author, a man whose brand of humor has led him to a career as a syndicated columnist.

If you are leaning toward a shorter book title, alliteration is an effective means of capturing a memorable quality to your book. The longest successful alliterative titles are no more than three words, which is pretty short, but there is something to be said for stickiness in a book title.

#1 NEW YORK TIMES BESTSELLER
GILLIAN FLYNN
AUTHOR OF
NOW AN HBO LIMITED SERIES
GONE GIRL
A NOVEL
"Ice-pick sharp . . . Spectacularly sneaky."
—NEW YORK TIMES

"A taut tale of ever deepening and quickening suspense."
—O, the Oprah Magazine
Everything I Never Told You
THE NEW YORK TIMES BESTSELLER
AUTHOR OF
LITTLE FIRES EVERYWHERE
CELESTE NG
A NOVEL
Celeste Ng

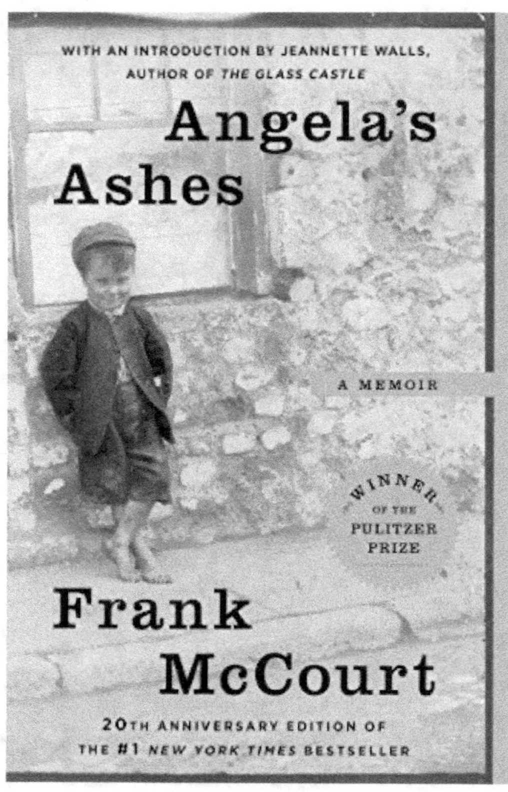

If at any point you would like my book marketing firm's help in promoting your book and creating your book title, please visit: http://www.book-marketing-expert.com where you can fill out our brief questionnaire telling us about your book, business and publishing goals.

NUMBERS, ALLUSIONS & IDIOMS

For as much as your prospective customers love reading beautiful words, using a number in the title can be very effective. There are quite a few reasons that explain this phenomenon.

For one thing, in a sea of words, numbers stand out.

Our brains are designed to pick out differences, however subtle, so using numbers capitalizes on that.

For nonfiction titles, numbers can be a clear way to drive home your book's value proposition. A book like *Three Cups of Tea: One Man's Mission to Promote Peace ... One School at a Time* by Greg Mortenson and David Oliver Relin, conveys a sense of simplicity and purpose on a most complicated issue, education. Everyone can emotionally identify with the concept of peace as it pertains to children.

One of the best-selling books ever, Mitch Albom's *The Five People You Meet in Heaven* creates a somber and pensive mood. If there are only five people, who are they?

I like using numbers in a book title especially when it's relevant and useful in describing what the book is about. A recent example that really works is *The 4-Hour Work Week* by Timothy Ferriss and his *4-Hour Body*. That number stops you in your tracks because it is shocking. How can you work just four hours a week? How can you have a good body in just four hours? Ferriss has capitalized on his branding of "4-Hour" and just published *The 4-Hour Chef*. He owns that number now. He's branded his name with "4-Hour" and will be able to incorporate it in his future work.

Using numbers in your title also saves on valuable title space. Amazon tends to shorten title displays on mobile devices, which is where more and more of your audience is shopping for books. Using 100 or 1,000 instead of the spelled numbers ensures more of your important keywords will appear on phones. Specifically, the number seven comes up big in book titles as well. Spelled out, the number seven is five letters, which is fairly long, but using the symbol 7 does more than save space. Psychologists say that the number seven possesses a great deal of allure and is by far people's favorite number. Knowing this is the case, it would be foolish not to optimize your title with an eye-catching symbol.

In fiction books, numbered titles have a sneaky way of conveying a lot about the story. J.R.R. Tolkien's epic fantasy classic, *The Two Towers* immediately brings up the idea of a conflict. A sense of singularity like *One For The Money* by best-selling author Janet Evanovich works as a play on the popular phrase but it also implies there is a lone character somewhere tied up in a conflict. That's a powerful draw.

Looking at *13 Reasons Why* by Jay Asher, a book that tackles everything facing tweens and teens like suicide, body image, shaming, and bullying, I don't think it would be as effective without naming the number of reasons. Asher is communicating volumes in that complicated number. Readers have to pick the book up to figure out for themselves whether that is a lot . . . or a little.

If your book comes as a part of a series, however long, adding that number to the title is crucial. One reason that should seem obvious is that book series are all the rage. When readers find something they enjoy reading, they want to know there will be more.

It also lends the book credibility. If you've got sixteen of these Jack Longtooth paranormal mysteries, readers feel emboldened to try the first. It's a matter of social proof.

Even if the book is the first in the series, on a deeper level, your addition of that number is like making a promise to the reader: "I hope you'll like this book. And if you do, *I promise there will be many more.*"

The key understanding with numbers is that they

help form relationships. Whether between characters or readers and facts, introducing those juxtapositions is an effective step.

THE LITERARY DEVICE known as allusion can be an effective tool in titling a book. If you are unfamiliar, allusion is an expression designed to call something to mind without referring to it directly.

How about an example?

As you might easily guess, allusions are often made to classic works. They need to be works that are so well known and easily recognizable that the reader effortlessly falls under their spell. If you think of what works are practically ubiquitous, the plays of William Shakespeare and the Bible come to mind. For a long stretch of history, these were the works of literature that *most people* knew.

Allusions to Shakespeare are bountiful in literature, from *Brave New World* by Aldous Huxley to *Infinite Jest* by David Foster Wallace to *The Winter of our Discontent* by John Steinbeck. These books are classic works of fiction, aided by their suggestive titles.

People don't know Shakespeare like they used to, you say? That statement is very likely true. Even if your prospective reader is unfamiliar with the source, the native poetry in the title phrase is undeniable. A *Brave New World* sets the stage for, in this case, a deep look at a dystopian future; the idea of *Infinite Jest* is one we are all drawn toward, especially its bittersweet sense of impossibility; what Steinbeck promises in his title is a deep exploration of a shared sadness within a family or community.

Biblical references can be more overt. If you look at

books like Toni Morrison's *Song of Solomon,* the title places the reader into a very specific part of the Holy Book. But a writer can think even simpler than that by alluding to Biblical language. *The Testament* by John Grisham and *Exodus* by Leon Uris were mega-sellers, and their titles merely hinted at the Bible. It seems reasonable to guess that Grisham and Uris could have used *other words* to title their books, synonyms for "testament" and "exodus," but the draw in making that connection proved far too powerful.

Alluding to commonly stated phrases is a way to use them to introduce your book. Successful books like *The Girl With The Dragon Tattoo* by Stieg Larsson, *The Girl Who Loved Tom Gordon* by Stephen King, and *The Girl Who Fell From The Sky* by Heidi Durrow follow a commonly used template: It introduces readers to the character and something unique about them.

It doesn't necessarily need to be a girl, either. *The Spy Who Came In From The Cold* by John le Carré and Oliver Sacks' *The Man Who Mistook His Wife for a Hat* follow a similar script. The main character is introduced to us, quickly followed by a taste of what makes them interesting.

Another commonly stated phrase in titles follows the "something's something" rule. *The Handmaid's Tale* by Margaret Atwood, *The Hitchhiker's Guide to the Galaxy* by Douglas Adams and *The Time Traveler's Wife* by Audrey Niffenegger all use a very simple formula familiar to readers.

The "blank of blank and blank" structure works well in many cases. Writers need look no further than George R.R. Martin's *A Song of Ice and Fire* series for evidence of that; the books launched a cultural landmark series as well as sparked a million internet chat room fights. *A Court of Thorns & Roses* is a wildly popular young adult fantasy series by Sarah J. Maas, and every title within that series uses a similar structure.

As we have seen in other title methodology, the key to success is in the connections and relationships created for the reader. These allusions stoke emotions.

WHAT IS AN IDIOM? An idiom is an expression with a different literal than figurative meaning. We hear idioms in everyday life, for example, "Don't cry over spilled milk" or "It takes two to tango."

Using idioms in your book title can make it memorable.

Why do we use idioms? Because they convey a powerful meaning in a few words. The best book titles use as few words as possible. It only makes sense that using an idiom with its "pre-packaged" meaning can be a perfect solution.

Here are some examples of books with idioms in their titles:

1. *Finders Keepers* by Stephen King
2. *Motor Mouth* by Janet Evanovich
3. *Cry Baby* by Gillian Flynn
4. *Mirror Image* by Sandra Brown
5. *Partners In Crime* by Agatha Christie

6. *Smoke Screen* by Sandra Brown
7. *Cut & Run* by Abigail Roux
8. *Fifty Shades of Grey* by E.L. James
9. *In Cold Blood* by Truman Capote
10. *When Pigs Fly* by Bob Sanchez
11. *One For The Money* by Janet Evanovich
12. *Catching Fire* by Suzanne Collins

THE "POWER OF FAMILIARITY" is also why idioms are used so often. A familiar phrase provides a comfort zone which is easily conveyed and understood by those who hear it. This is why if you choose an idiom for your book title, people may believe they've "heard of" that book. If they've heard of it, then it must be good, or else why would someone be telling them about that book?

How many times have you heard someone say, "Oh I just heard about this new book"? They can't remember where or who they heard it from, just that it must be good.

Often, they are simply repeating a talk show host or something from an author interview. This is why word of mouth is the best advertising—and it all starts by having a memorable title.

Even though idioms can be very effective, there are at least a few handy rules you need to follow in order to make them work. Using a familiar saying can be useful, but employing an overused phrase can cause people to gloss over it like a worn-out cliché. You need to consider your audience.

It goes without saying that idioms can be confusing for non-English speakers. Different ethnicities use different terms, so it is important to be familiar with your target audience. For example, the Irish idiom "It's throwing cobblers' knives" means in English, "It's raining cats and dogs!"

Keep in mind that idioms may work better for certain genres, too. Children's book authors are notorious for using idioms in their titles. There are a few reasons for this.

First, children tend to be attracted to titles that are simple and fun. For example, *There's a Frog in My Throat* or *It's Raining Cats and Dogs* are more likely to catch a child's attention than a title meant to draw readers in by attempting to be creative and artistic. The opposite goes for thriller and mystery books. A book with the title of *Dead Tired* is bound to grab the attention of someone looking for a thriller/mystery book. It gives the reader a glimpse of what is to come.

THE NO.1 NEW YORK TIMES BESTSELLER
THE 4-HOUR WORK WEEK
ESCAPE THE 9-5,
LIVE ANYWHERE AND
JOIN THE NEW RICH
TIMOTHY FERRISS
EXPANDED &
UPDATED

BRAVE NEW WORLD
ALDOUS HUXLEY

THE #1 NEW YORK TIMES
AND INTERNATIONAL BESTSELLER
NOW IN 31 LANGUAGES
THIRTEEN REASONS
WHY
A NOVEL BY
JAY ASHER
EERIE, BEAUTIFUL
AND DEVASTATING
CHICAGO TRIBUNE
"A MYSTERY, EULOGY,
CEREMONY"
—SHERMAN ALEXIE

UTILIZING A SERIES TITLE

"I write a new title, sometimes a phrase from the work. Then, I Google it and discover twenty-seven other authors have beat me to it. (Always Google your title.) So, I change a few words. Agonize. Change a few more. Sometimes, I go back to the journal and find the perfect title has been there all along."

— Anne R. Allen, author of the best-selling *Camilla Randall* comedy-mystery series

Having a series title to go alongside your book title is a great way to drum up interest and bring new and returning readers to your books.

Back to our example of *Once Bitten*. You're afforded up to two hundred spaces for your book title. You can do a lot to build your book's searchability by adding a keyword-rich series title to the listing.

Once Bitten: A Sweetneck High Paranormal Romance Mystery.

The series title allows you to pull in searchers who may be looking for your series (because they've heard of it from someone they know), but the subtitle also uses interesting keywords: paranormal, romance, and mystery. Another word that draws interest is series, because readers love series.

Subtitles are very effective in drawing reader interest. Even casual browsers of your listing will stop to consider what sounds like a cool, campy, interesting journey into a freaky high school.

DOUGLAS ADAMS
The Hitchhiker's
Guide to the
Galaxy
a novel

If at any point you would like my book marketing firm's help in promoting your book and creating your book title, please visit: http://www.book-marketing-expert.com where you can fill out our brief questionnaire telling us about your book, business and publishing goals.

PEN NAMES

— Kristen Kieffer, author of the *The Books of Maveryn* series and *The Astral* series

Pen names have been a rich tradition for hundreds of years for fiction writers. You may be surprised to learn that some authors have more than ten pen names. Here is the very simple reason why pen names have been and continue to be widely used: Many authors believe that their name can affect how their audience sees them and even affect their book sales. For an explanation of this subject we need to dive in and explore the world of branding.

First, let's be clear about your byline. Your name is synonymous with your book's title. In the example of your paranormal romance novel, *Once Bitten,* your byline pops up in your reader's mind. You are synonymous with your writing. It is as much a part of your brand as your voice.

Branding ends up being quite a touchy subject for a lot of authors. If you go to a writer's conference and listen to the talk around the bar, you'll hear a lot of griping about branding, and it's easy to see why. Most writers pour their heart and soul into developing their characters and story. They work through draft after draft to get those very difficult aspects right. By the time they get out into the world, the last thing any writer wants to think about is their branding strategy.

However, it is vitally important to consider. I'm not going to go on about platform or how to engage in social media, but the author looking at a long-term career needs to understand that their name is their brand.

Stephen King is the master of modern horror. Sue Grafton is synonymous with mystery books.

If you're looking at your writing career as a long-term proposition (as you absolutely should), then your name becomes a very valuable asset to you. After a half-dozen successful military thrillers, you may be mentioned right alongside, uhm, uhm . . . who is that guy? Tom Clancy, right. Of course, I'm talking about Tom Clancy.

But let's just say that halfway through your very successful run of military thrillers you end up optioning one of your books to a movie production company. Now that you have your audience, you've gotten a taste of significant money—seven-figure Hollywood cash for your stories—you want to take a break and get the inspiration to write something else. Let's say you have that paranormal romance itching to get out.

At that juncture, your name is synonymous in the reading world with military thrillers. If you add a paranormal romance title to your bookshelf, you're going to confuse your audience. What is *Once Bitten* doing on the same shelf with these other books? There may be some crossover between military thriller readers and those of juvenile vampire romances, but it's doubtful.

In this instance, going in the direction of a pen name is the right choice for you. Within your Author Central page, Amazon allows writers to create and monitor a number of concurrent pen names. Using a couple of pen names is hardly more difficult than one.

Writers need to be aware of the market. They also need to be aware of their own need and desire to diversify. It's perfectly OK to dive in and try something else, as long as you go about that reinvention process the right way.

ONE OF MY book marketing clients served as a Navy Seal in the Iraq War. When he returned, he set out to write a book about his war experiences.

The author was concerned that extremists living in America would be offended and angered by his controversial book and come after him or his family. So, to protect his personal safety and that of his family, my client wrote under the pen name Chuck Bravedy.

The fact that Bravedy's name was not in the phone book garnered some attention from the Pentagon. They actually called me to inquire because they did not have his name in their files. The Pentagon was concerned because they want to keep phonies from impersonating military officials.

The publishers of the *Harry Potter* series of books by J.K. Rowling were unsure if her target audience of preteen boys would accept wizard stories written by a woman. Because of this, they encouraged her to use her initials instead of her real name, which is Joanne Rowling. The "K" in J.K. came from her grandmother's name, Kathleen, and she's been known as J.K. Rowling ever since.

Known as one of the most famous comic book writers in the world, Stan Lee's real name was Stanley Martin Lieber. He initially decided to publish under Stan Lee because he thought he would eventually transition to more serious work and wanted to use his real name if and when that time came. Once he realized that he was destined to stay a comic book writer, he legally changed his name to Stan Lee.

One client I represented who asked my advice about using a pen name was a former CIA operative. He was concerned about the impact a pen name would have on promoting his book. He wondered whether radio and TV interviewers would be willing to use the pen name during an interview, or if they would insist on using his birth name.

Some of his CIA friends had published books and used their real names without problems. To cover his bases while he decided, the former CIA officer went ahead and registered web domains under his real name *and* his pen name. After talking with him about the options, my client decided to use his real name.

I also have represented authors who used a pen name because they had a past they were not proud of and wanted to protect their family members and loved ones from public embarrassment.

From a marketing standpoint, if your real-life identity is associated with a business and you want the book to promote your business, or vice versa, then a pen name should not be used. But if you are successful and don't want that success threatened by pursuing an avocation of writing, then a pen name would be in order. Although most marketing challenges created by pen names can be overcome, the implications need to be examined carefully before publishing.

A list of the many reasons for using a pen name include:

• To avoid embarrassment
• For personal safety or security
• If you write under more than one genre
• If your name is hard to pronounce or spell
• If your name is not marketable
• If your name conflicts with the name of another author
• To hide gender (a male writing in predominantly female genre, etc.)
• To avoid confusing readers if you are well known in another field

IF YOU WANT to hide from the public, then a pen name is fine. But, if it's not important, why bother? So, my vote is to use your own name. Here are just a few points to ponder:

• Use your real name if you are not trying to hide from anyone
• Use your real name to brand it for speaking gigs or consulting assignments
• Use your real name if you are planning to write a series of books
• Use your real name so acquaintances can better locate your published works
• A real name builds trust and confidence among readers
• It's far easier to brand a real name than a pen name
• Expertise is validated by an individual's real-life experience
• Long-term loyalty with readers is easier to build with real name

HERE IS EVEN MORE interesting information I've obtained from librarians and employees at book stores: If there is a popular author whose work is similar to yours, why not select a pen name beginning with the same letter as that author's last name? Since most books are filed by genre and then the author's last name, selecting a pen name with the same letter puts you in close proximity to their books.

Someone searching for that author could "stumble" upon your book and decide to take a look. Radio stations have done it for years—selecting their location on the "dial" near highly rated stations so they could benefit from the proximity of that popular station. Crafty? Perhaps. But do you want to sell books or not?

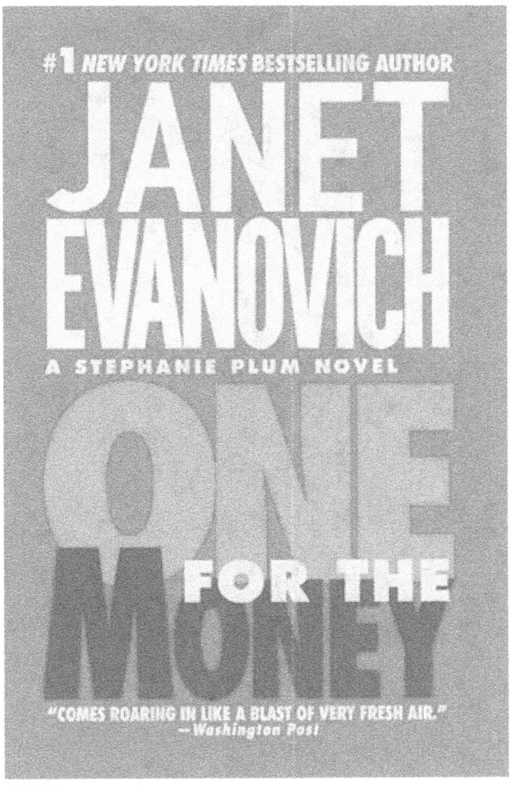

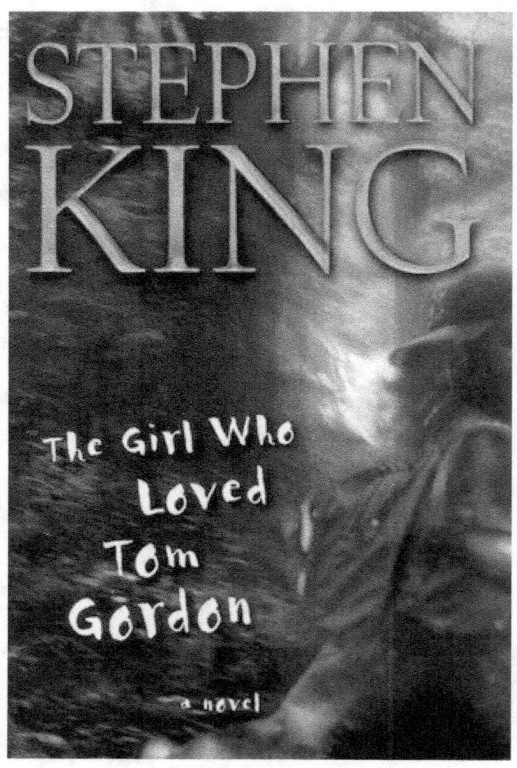
STEPHEN
KING
The Girl Who
Loved
Tom
Gordon
a novel

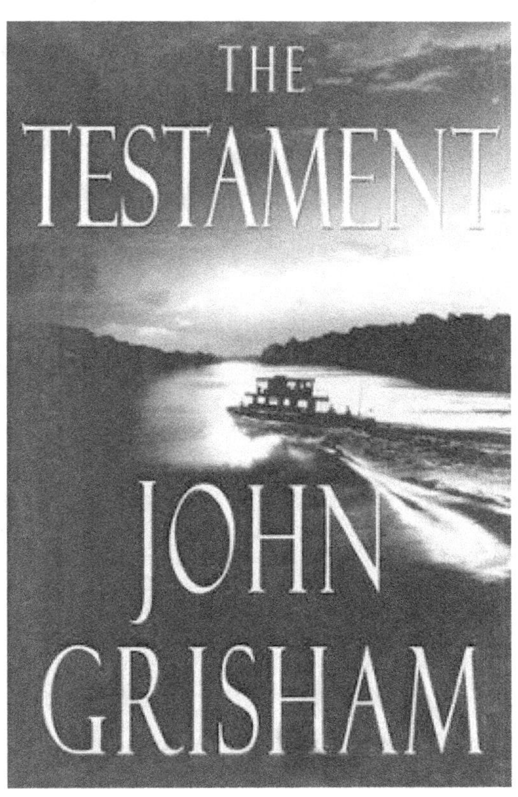
THE
TESTAMENT
JOHN
GRISHAM

GENRE MASH-UPS, PARODY & CONTRADICTION

"Don't stop with studying the length of best-selling books. Look at titles similar to what you want to write. You will find extensive book databases at Goodreads.com and WorldCat.org. Both of these sites list most books published in every genre. Take time to list ten books that are similar to yours. What is the length of each title? Your book title length should be somewhere in the neighborhood."

— Molly Blaisdell, children's book author

You can be sure of one thing. Your prospective reader, wherever they are, will probably look at a lot of books before they get to yours, even if you're already on the first page of Amazon. That reality isn't a way of saying that your cover needs work or your premise needs yet another polish. The reality is that there are a lot of books out there.

Once someone has clicked through page after page after page of books on the dizzyingly large Amazon Kindle Store, they're a bit bleary-eyed and they probably need something to jolt their attention.

In 2009, Seth Grahame-Smith published the parody novel *Pride and Prejudice and Zombies*. It was as unlikely a novel to hit the *New York Times* Best Seller list, captivate audiences, and turn into a major motion picture as ever there was. Why was the book such a breakout hit? There is a genius to the book's whole premise: It cleverly capitalizes on two seemingly inexhaustible obsessions: the work of Jane Austen and zombies.

Focusing on the title (the subject of this book after all), Grahame-Smith proves a double stroke of inspiration. The title mashes up two very different genres (at least to the casual reader), literature and horror, on its way to creating a third all its own. Paired with the now classic cover image, it had all the makings of a best seller in place. A best seller and a sequel. What could be a better outcome than that?

There are those who might think that a title like *Pride and Prejudice and Zombies* is a cheap way to draw readers. Fair enough. That may be a worthy observation.

But the critics were rather bullish on the book. Many writers across the country applauded the small publisher for not only being bold enough to publish a book of such high-minded parody, but to give it an exciting title.

Jennifer Schuessler of *The New York Times* said, "Publishers in search of a marketing hook aren't above trumpeting even their most middling wares as a mix of Dickens, Chekhov, and Dan Brown. This year, a small publishing house in Philadelphia hit on a more effective formula: Take some Jane Austen, add a healthy dollop of gore, and start counting the money." Translation: the experiment worked.

What makes the mash-up in the title so brilliant is that it almost immediately puts the reader onto the tone, voice, subject, and mood of the book. This is going to have all of the silly manners of Austen's England with a horde of bloodthirsty zombies to spice things up a bit. And right away, you know it's going to be funny, too.

Grahame-Smith wasn't the only author to recognize the capacity for success with this particular formula. Other similar fiction projects include books like *Abraham Lincoln, Vampire Hunter*; *Sense and Sensibility and Sea Monsters*; and my personal favorite, *Android Karenina*.

If you're writing fiction that takes chances, if you're looking to find a unique place for your book, a mash-up title may be the right choice for you.

THIS TYPE of title can work very well in nonfiction and children's books as well. The key for authors is to recognize the core appeal within the language: mixed expectations. Jolting your reader into paying attention to your book over others on the Amazon page can be a critical aspect of your success.

Nonfiction book titles like *Freakonomics* or *Thinking, Fast and Slow* or *Everything Is Horrible and Wonderful* (all incredibly popular, best-selling titles) are successful in taking two concepts and crashing them together. In the case of the first, we all know what economics are and we (probably) know a few freaks, too. Put two familiar things together and you get Freakonomics, an entirely new concept that paints a pretty funny picture.

You want to pick that book up, right? Seven million other readers felt the same way. At least 100 other books about economics came out that same year, and all of those together didn't sell as many copies.

You can add to that list *Are You There, Vodka? It's Me, Chelsea* by the irrepressible Chelsea Handler. One of the most audaciously titled books ever written, the always entertaining Handler took the title of a well-known children's book (*Are You There, God? It's Me, Margaret*) and gave it her own boozy spin. The title is blatant, out there, and oh-so Chelsea.

One of my favorites is the cleverly titled *Cloudy With a Chance of Meatballs*, a children's book by Judi Barrett. It is an obvious parody of a weather report and a funny one at that. Deeper still though, what Barrett achieved with this title (besides a hilarious image) is the suggestion of an emotional journey. Cloudy implies drab or sad. The chance of meatballs tells us that there is some fun in store. Maybe by the end of the book, everything is going to be OK.

The success of *Freakonomics* and *Are You There, Vodka? It's Me, Chelsea* lies in more than just gaudy sales numbers, though. In 2005, economist Steven Levitt and Stephen J. Dubner took basic economics, married it with pop culture, and fifteen years later, that has spawned television properties, radio and a consultation gig for its authors. By every measure, that is a successful nonfiction book, owed in no small part to the genius in the title of the book.

As for Handler, although she was probably always destined for success, the book helped catapult her into a new stratosphere for a female comic. From movies to television, she's everywhere.

Not to forget *Cloudy With a Chance of Meatballs,* Barrett's book was a smash success with readers. Almost thirty years after its publication, the story went through a wildly popular film adaptation, a sequel, and a television series to boot.

Successful parodies have also boldly tipped off the end of the book, too. Just look at David Wong's irreverent horror classic *John Dies at the End* or the more dramatic *By The Time You Read This, I'll Be Dead* by Julie Anne Peters. Spoiling the ending is not only a way of spinning expectations, but it presents a critical question in the reader's mind: How did they get here?

A little humor goes a long way.

I would be remiss if I wrote a book about titles without making mention of *Eats, Shoots & Leaves: The Zero Tolerance Approach to Punctuation* by Lynne Truss. On the back of a title that was, in fact, the punchline to a joke, Truss managed to hit a culture-penetrating best seller with a book about grammar.

WE ARE all drawn in some way to contrast. This is a natural way our brains work, looking and listening for things that don't make sense or contradict logic.

You can use this when coming up with a title for your book, too. Think of one of the classics of world literature, Leo Tolstoy's doorstop novel *War and Peace.* This capitalizes on one of the most staggering contrasts in worldview.

Examples from a more contemporary sense include Dan Brown who used stark contrasts in titling his best-selling novel, *Angels & Demons,* as did John Gray in his self-help classic, *Men Are from Mars, Women Are from Venus.* When Ellen DeGeneres released *Seriously … I'm Kidding,* she drew attention to the book with that humorous contradiction, but also set the tone for her book that works well for her unique brand of humor.

These titles are effective because they tease our brain's natural need to pick out contrasts. But they also, again, imply critical relationships within the book with relative ease. War and peace. Angels and demons. The interplanetary differences between men and women.

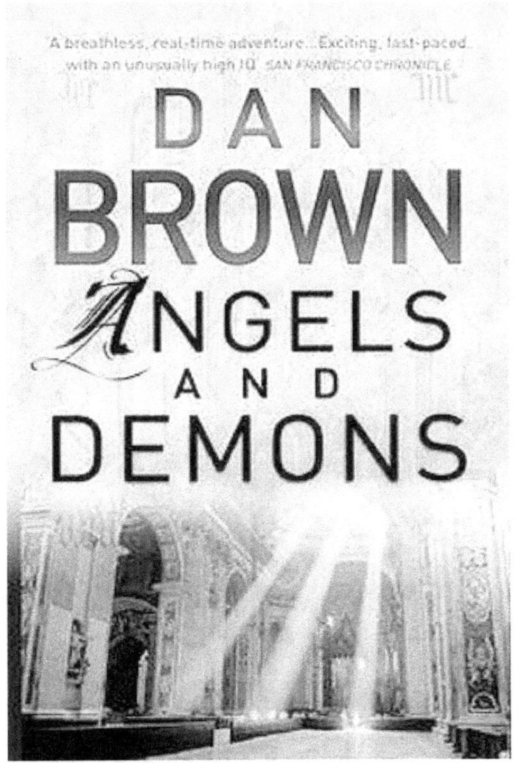
A breathless, real-time adventure...Exciting, fast-paced
with an unusually high IQ SAN FRANCISCO CHRONICLE
DAN
BROWN
ANGELS
AND
DEMONS

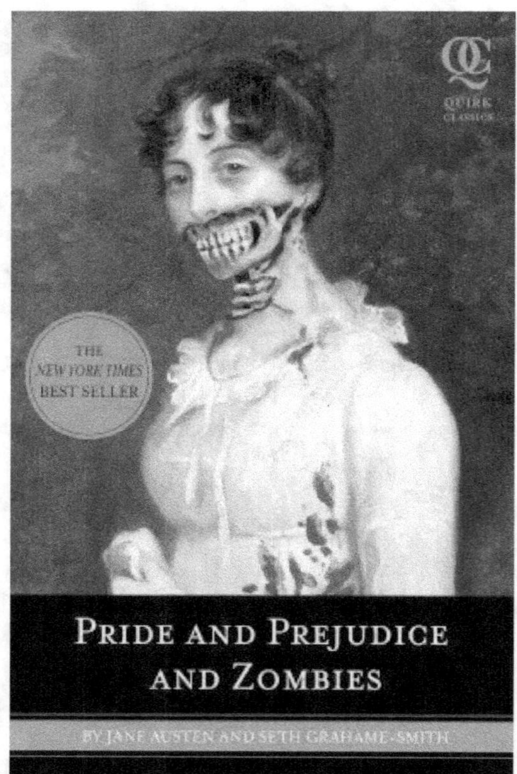
QC
QUIRK
CLASSICS

THE
NEW YORK TIMES
BEST SELLER

PRIDE AND PREJUDICE
AND ZOMBIES

BY JANE AUSTEN AND SETH GRAHAME-SMITH

If at any point you would like my book marketing firm's help in promoting your book and creating your book title, please visit: http://www.book-marketing-expert.com where you can fill out our brief questionnaire telling us about your book, business and publishing goals.

PROFANITY

If you are offended by four-letter words and other profanity, skip this chapter. Why? The use of profanity in book titles has hit a new high, and some would say, new low.

This chapter may come as a bit of a surprise to some readers, but yes, a little profanity in your book's title can go a very long way toward its ultimate success. I'm not including it merely for shock value. Instead, I'm including this chapter here because shock value can work wonders.

Remember that memorability is a highly sought-after quality in a book title. The last thing that any author, whether new or established, can afford is to have their book forgotten.

I know what you might be thinking though. Giving your book a title with profanity will make prospective readers think it's dirty. Maybe it will scare away some. But will it steer away too many?

I suppose that initial caution may be true. If you look at the sales numbers however, there is clearly another side to the notion. Some incredibly successful books give the first impression of a potty mouth.

In the psychology and self-help space (as well as a decent dose of humor) Mark Manson drew in curious readers with *The Subtle Art of Not Giving A F*ck: A Counterintuitive Approach to Living a Good Life*. The message in the title is quite clear, right? Manson is challenging his readers to pick up his book. He is daring them to open the cover and see if he really has the secrets to living a good life. There is also a clear suggestion of irreverence in the tone. Some people don't care. Mark Manson is selling a book to people who don't give a fuck.

I remember running into Mark Manson at his publisher's booth while attending Book Expo a few years ago in Chicago. I am no prude, but I was blown away by the title of his book and the overall acceptance of it within the publishing world. It helped that Manson was a published writer, but still, it was an eye-grabbing title. Then his next book title played on that as well with, *Everything Is F*cked: A Book About Hope*. Manson has great courage, but he also no doubt has a sense of humor, and it was his book that really opened the floodgates to the increase of profanity in titles.

Confessions of a Prairie Bitch: How I Survived Nellie Oleson And Learned to Love Being Hated was a well-received memoir written by the actress who played the titular *Little House on the Prairie* goody two shoes tattle-tale. Everyone knows her. She's infamous. Alison Arngrim knows very well what people of a certain generation think of her. What could be a better title? She jumps right out, acknowledging her public persona, and plays it off for a tone of redemption.

The humor genre is huge in books right now. It is a place where new and established comics and performers make inroads with new fans. Profanity is hilarious, right? Look at books like *Go The F*ck To Sleep* or *Sh*t My Dad Says*. Although there are underlying appeals here, namely the irony that they are a children's book and the popular Twitter handle respectively, the brands are almost purely in the profane title.

On a more serious note, profanity is a way to drum up emotions. It can be used to hit vulnerable readers over the head. In some instances, especially nonfiction titles, the confrontation of a profane title sells a sense of alienation or a morbid tone. If you look at books like the pro-feminist *Cunt: A Declaration of Independence* or *Bastards: A Memoir,* the tone becomes very clear right away. While they explore serious topics, they're not willing to pull punches in the process.

While profanity may have the slight drawback of turning off a few of your prospective readers, the potential benefits clearly outweigh those. This strategy is bold. It draws attention.

I also think that it has the benefit of weeding out iffy

readers. If you click to buy any of the books described above, you pretty much know what you're getting into.

The key to successfully using profanity is to know that it isn't a fit for everything—even when the genre seems to be a fit. It must match the overall tone of the book.

Profanity is almost always used in nonfiction books. It's a no-no in most genres of fiction (outside of westerns which use "bastard" disproportionately) especially romance and erotica. But if you have that just-right, irreverent manuscript, getting down and dirty may be the right choice for your book.

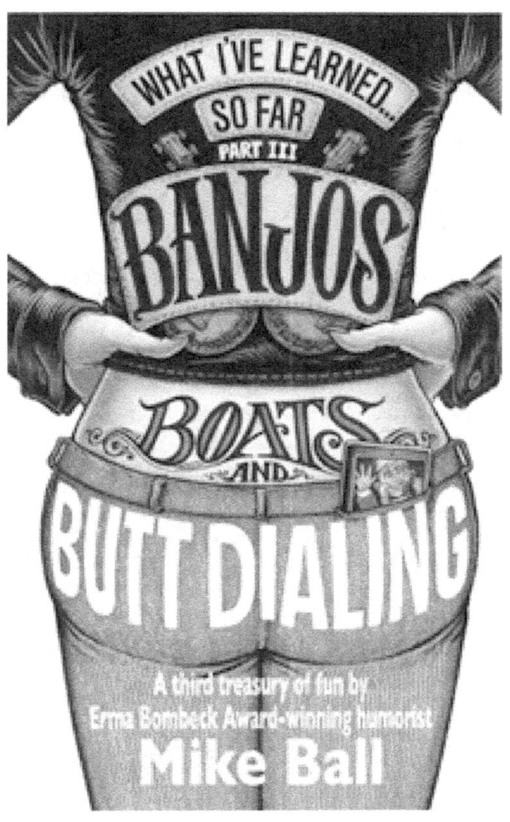
WHAT I'VE LEARNED...
SO FAR
PART III
BANJOS
BOATS
AND
BUTT DIALING
A third treasury of fun by
Erma Bombeck Award-winning humorist
Mike Ball

OVER THREE MILLION COPIES SOLD
THE SUBTLE ART OF NOT GIVING A F*CK
#1
New York
Times
Bestseller
A COUNTERINTUITIVE APPROACH
TO LIVING A GOOD LIFE
MARK MANSON

ALISON ARNGRIM
CONFESSIONS OF A
PRAIRIE BITCH

RESOURCES

As this book lays out, coming up with a great title can be easier said than done. There is some good news, however. There are resources out there to help your process along.

A book title generator is one example of a tool you can use to jump-start your creative juices and come up with a compelling, attention-grabbing title that speaks to your audience. This may be the key to increasing sales, interest, and impact. There are various generators available online. Here are a few you may want to consider.

PORTENT'S CONTENT IDEA GENERATOR: Simply enter the subject of your book and this generator gives you some ideas. You can continue to click the arrow until you find a title that piques your interest.

KOPYWRITING KOURSE BOOK NAME GENERATOR: Once you type in your subject, it creates a list of hundreds of book titles. Chances are, you'll find one (or a few) that suits your book.

AWESOME TITLES TITLE GENERATOR: Believe it or not, this generator can open your eyes to 700 catchy titles. Enter the main keyword and you'll get three pages worth of ideas.

SELFPUBLISHING.COM NONFICTION BOOK TITLE GENERATOR: If you're in need of a title for your nonfiction book, this generator is invaluable. Enter a word that describes its topic. After you click "Generate," it'll deliver some good options.

RUGGENBERG TITLE GENERATOR: Get six titles at one time with this generator. All you have to do is click "Give me some titles," sit back, relax, and allow the tool to work its magic.

ADAZING BOOK TITLE GENERATOR: This book title generator promises to give you "perfect titles in less than 30 seconds." It's a bit more involved than other generators because it asks you to select your genre and type in details like the occupation of the protagonist and main character's goal.

SERENDIPITY FANTASY NOVEL TITLE GENERATOR: For a simple generator for your fantasy book, this is a solid pick. Continue to click "Another" until you see what you're looking for.

SUMO KICKASS HEADLINE GENERATOR: This allows you to choose the type of title you want: A numbered list, how-to, controversial, playful, etc. Once you do, it'll ask you to enter a topic and desired outcome before it spits out an option.

WRITING EXERCISES STORY TITLE GENERATOR: With the Writing Exercises Story Title Generator, you can click back and forth between the "Adjective" and "Noun" buttons to create a unique story title.

CLICK HERE to get a list of links to these book title generators.

AS AN AUTHOR, you know that a book title can mean the difference between a best seller and one that stays on the shelf for good. With these book title generators and my expert advice on how to find the perfect title, you can steer your latest work toward incredible success.

If at any point you would like my book marketing firm's help in promoting your book and creating your book title, please visit: http://www.book-marketing-expert.com where you can fill out our brief questionnaire telling us about your book, business and publishing goals.

CONCLUSION

"The title should contain some dominant word which clearly indicates the subject of the book . . . If human nature can be put into the title, well and good. Every effort should be made to tie up the book with real life, or with the average person's desire for romance, adventure, and fun."

— E. Haldeman-Julius, the head of Haldeman-Julius Publications and creator of a series of pamphlets known as "Little Blue Books," total sales of which has run into the hundreds of millions of copies.

In this book, we have discussed how finding the right title for your book is critical to its success. Previous chapters covered a myriad of approaches to getting the right title, from defining keywords/keyword phrases, to discussions of everything from poetry to profanity. Here is another thing to consider.

As a book publicist, I understand your first attempt at titling your book may not work out. Throughout the course of literary history, numerous successful books have been retitled. I bet you didn't know that George Orwell's dystopian novel *1984* started out as *The Last Man in Europe* or that *Dracula* was originally titled *Dead/Un-Dead*. Can you imagine? Before Harper Lee gave us *To Kill a Mockingbird,* she had first thought to title the book *Atticus*.

The point is, anything is possible in the world of publishing. If you've just finished reading this book and you have a regretful book title in your catalog, consider going back and giving it a new name. After all, *Atlas Shrugged* probably would not be one of the most popular (and controversial) books of the last century if Ayn Rand had stuck with the generic, *Strike*.

ABOUT THE AUTHOR

By now, you should grasp the reality that your book's title is among the key elements critical to its long- term success. If you take the time and utilize the tools laid out for you here and choose the right search engine-tailored title, your book will have an inside edge in turning big sales at the top of the Amazon rankings. Choose the wrong title and your book languishes in obscurity.

When it comes to which path your book takes, the choice is up to you, the author.

Writing a book is tough. You know that already. You've done it.

Being a book publicist, I know that marketing a successful publication is difficult, too, make no mistake about that. There is a lot that goes into making your publishing journey a successful one.

If you want to work with a professional marketer and

publicist on a plan to take your book all the way to the top, look no further. My book marketing campaigns help drive sales and build sustainable careers. In addition to assisting you in finding the right title for your book, I can get it into the hands of print, broadcast, and electronic media nationwide.

Don't get lost in the jungle of book marketing. Whether this book is your first or fiftieth, get found by your readers on Amazon. Contact me and let's begin the conversation.

Scott Lorenz
President
Westwind Communications
Office: 734-667-2090
scottlorenz@westwindcos.com
http://www.Book-Marketing-Expert.com
Follow me on Twitter at: @aBookPublicist

FIVE STAR REVIEWS FOR BOOK TITLE
GENERATOR

"Book Publicist Scott Lorenz gives you the ABCs and XYZs of picking the perfect title for that book you have put your heart into. It's required reading for aspiring or experienced writers."

John Kelly
Detroit Free Press

"This is an indispensable, first-rate adjunct to the art of writing – and selling- your book."

Dr. Grady Harp
Amazon Top 50 Hall of Fame Reviewer

"Authors owe it to themselves to 'turn-every-stone' to make sure they have the best possible book title. It's critical to the success of any book... unless you are already famous... then it doesn't matter."

Mike Ball
Erma Bombeck Award-Winning Author

"Revealed! The secret behind choosing a great title for your book can be found in Book Title Generator... it's essential reading for authors... before they title their book!"

Susan Keefe
Midwest Book Review

"A thoughtful collection of techniques and tips for naming a book. I highly recommend it."

**Pamela Gossiaux,
Bestselling Author, Russo Romantic Mysteries**

"Authors Stop! Don't Pass GO! You must read this book BEFORE you title your book. Don't make that fateful mistake of mistitling your book!"

Jess Todtfeld, **Author Media Secrets, Former TV Producer for NBC, ABC and FOX**

"I get HUNDREDS of books a year from hopeful authors. The title has to catch my attention or I pass. If I were an author I'd read Book Title Generator."

Chris Cordani, **Executive Producer, Money Matters on WABC-AM, New York**